10-25-76

A CATECHISM

FOR

DIVORCED CATHOLICS

A *CATECHISM*

FOR

DIVORCED CATHOLICS

by
James J. Rue, Ph.D. and Louise Shanahan

ABBEY PRESS ● *St. Meinrad, Indiana* 47577 ● 1976

First Printing—July, 1976
Second Printing—August 1976

Published by Abbey Press
St. Meinrad, IN 47577

Library of Congress Cataloging in Publication Data
Rue, James J.
  A catechism for divorced catholics.

  1. Divorcees. 2. Marriage—Catholic Church. 3. Divorce (Canon
law) I. Shanahan, Louise, joint author. II. Title.
HQ823.R79   261.8'34'284   76-16170
ISBN 0-87029-063-0
Printed in the United States of America

TABLE OF CONTENTS

1943520

35820

Preliminary Statement

I have reviewed the book written by Louise Shanahan and Dr. James Rue, and would recommend it to those persons who find themselves in the position of being divorced, and desiring some guidelines whereby they can gain hope and promise for themselves. The Church must address itself to persons in this situation. This book certainly is a move in that direction. It is written with sensitivity and insight.

Father Clifford Parker
Associate Director
Marriage Tribunal
Archdiocese of Los Angeles
Los Angeles, Califorina

PREFACE

There are at least five million divorced Catholics presently (1975) in the United States. This figure, furthermore, does not take into account the millions of minor children whose future lives will be affected by the decisions one or both of their parents make about their allegiance to the faith.

This significant body of Catholic men and women is increasing year by year as a steady erosion of Judeo-Christian tradition occurs in our secular society. These men and women search desperately for a sense of direction and purpose to mend their broken lives.

The lethal infiltration of anti-Christian ethics has inundated our society to such a degree that Catholics have found themselves swamped and confused by the new morality which promises happiness and freedom and flexible marriage and no-fault divorce. The "ouchless" band-aid of permissive morality has not provided soothing relief for all the problems following a dissolution of marriage. It merely masks the agony and delays recovery.

Millions of Catholics and other Christians are searching for answers, direction, and meaning to their lives subsequent to divorce. The human desolation following divorce is unimaginable to those who have not lived through the experience personally.

It is, however, in the midst of this crucible that the divorced Catholic gropes toward answers that will give his life deeper meaning and direction. The feelings of despair, anger, loneliness, sexual frustration, and bewilderment can be transmuted.

In our book *The Divorced Catholic*, we indicated our belief in alternatives to divorce. Among these are: (1) premarital education and counseling, (2) counseling during marital crisis, (3) post-divorce counseling, and (4) Church-sponsored marriage education programs.

We believe such programs will reverse the divorce trend among Catholics provided that in each community these programs are utilized by those individuals most in need of such help.

Availability of programs and dissemination of factual information, particularly among our young people, will reaffirm the teachings of Christ with respect to the sacramental nature of marriage and all its concomitant obligations.

We believe, moreover, for those Catholics who are divorced, that there are significant areas of misunderstanding and lack of accurate information on specific religious issues, divorce, and nullity of marriage which need to be clarified.

A surprising number of Catholics seem to believe erroneously, for example, that they are automatically excommunicated from the Church following divorce. Lack of correct information fueled by powerful emotional responses to divorce may deter the confused Catholic from inquiry and the practice of his or her faith.

We believe that a catechism of basic religious information is needed by the millions of divorced Catholics who are searching for assurance that they, too, are members of the Mystical Body of Christ.

It is our intention then to aid in some measure those divorced Catholics who feel as if they are displaced and "homeless" persons within the Church, those who visualize themselves on the "outside" looking "in," and those who cling with valiant allegiance to a religious faith that is now only gradually acknowledging their ever-increasing numbers.

There is an abundant Christian life after divorce which Christ promises to all those who will follow Him. It is available to all those Catholics who will take the time and energy to pursue answers and opportunities within the Church.

Will you accept this invitation?

ACKNOWLEDGEMENTS

We wish to express our sincere gratitude to Father Timothy O'Connell, Director of the Family Life Bureau of Los Angeles, and Father Clifford Parker, Associate Director of the Marriage Tribunal of the Archdiocese of Los Angeles, for their helpful suggestions and factual contributions on the subject of nullity of marriage.

We are also grateful to Fran Miller of the Judeans, an organization for divorced Catholic women, officially recognized by the Archdiocese of San Francisco; it was Fran who gave us the idea and encouragement to write this catechism-handbook.

The Judean Society is now international with chapters in various dioceses in the United States and abroad. These dedicated women who are divorced offer a variety of services including: workshops, retreats, shared prayers and various newsletters and publications. There are social activities to provide members with opportunities for relaxation. The Judeans meet in small neighborhood groups offering personal comfort and inspiration to one another in self/help, mutual/help programs.

At the request of Joseph T. McGucken, Archbishop of San Francisco, California, on May 9, 1975, the Holy Father, Pope Paul VI, blessed and proclaimed the Judean Society, Inc., a "True and Just Apostolate."

For further information on the Judean Society write:
Fran Miller
1075 Space Park Way #336
Mountain View, CA 94040

QUESTIONS AND ANSWERS

Does the Catholic Church believe in divorce?

The Catholic Church does not believe in divorce, but permits it when circumstances require civil proceedings as a legal solution.

Divorce is provided for in civil law so as to protect the legal rights of women and minor children. However, as federal and state laws begin to recognize equality of the sexes, and there is some possibility of a national divorce law, legislation may be enacted to reflect this equality. There may be instances where men as well as women will be awarded alimony and child custody and support depending, of course, on the individual circumstances of the case.

The Church presently recognizes the need for civil divorce in the sense that certain human rights, particularly those of women and children, might be forfeited if divorce was not available as a means of legal protection. Under certain state laws, for example, where the husband prevails as the manager and director of family assets, it is possible for a wife to have her share mismanaged or squandered, and she has no recourse, except the civil law, for correcting these inequities.

Thus the Church permits divorce to protect certain human God-given rights which might conceivably be destroyed through an intolerable marriage.

Civil law represents a continuing state of flux while the philosophical position of the Church is based on a concern for human happiness within the context of eternal salvation. Hence the Church understands that divorce in itself is merely one stage of growth in terms of the individual's struggle toward spiritual perfection and union with God.

Explain the word "divorce" in terms of Catholic doctrine.

Divorce is a judgment or decree handed down in a civil court declaring the dissolution of a marriage. It is related to civil law, not to moral law.

The decree handed down in a civil court may enable a Catholic to petition a diocesan marriage tribunal for a nullity of marriage.

Such an ecclesiastical annulment declares that a marriage was null and void from the beginning because of some impediment when the man and woman gave their consent at the time of marriage.

In the Old Testament, Moses sanctioned divorce according to certain conditions. However, in the New Testament, as it is recorded in the Gospel of St. Matthew, Christ raised marriage to the dignity of a sacrament (19:3-6).

Christ said, "Whoever puts away his wife and marries another, commits adultery against her; and if the wife puts away her husband and marries another, she commits adultery" (Mark 10:2-12).

The Catholic Church teaches that no state authority (civil court) can grant a divorce thereby permitting one or both parties to enter into a second marriage. This means that although a civil divorce may be recognized by the Church for purposes of protecting the life and property of one of the mates, frequently the wife, and the children, this recognition in itself is not a tacit permission to marry again.

Divorce, however, is permitted when there is no other solution to an intolerable marriage, but this permission does not grant the right to one or both mates to enter into a second marriage.

At the present time, the only conditions under which another marriage may be contracted is to have had the first marriage declared null and void, or dissolved by a special ecclesiastical privilege (Pauline Privilege of Favor of the Faith), according to the processes employed by the proper Archdiocesan Matrimonial Tribunal.

Thus a Catholic in these circumstances is free to marry. The secular world may interpret this act as entering into a second marriage, but according to the doctrines of the Catholic Church, such a marriage is a first one in the sight of God.

Is conscience a satisfactory guide to divorce?

The Catholic who is contemplating divorce is frequently troubled by his conscience because he* has been taught that divorce is prohibited by the Church, although it is permitted in certain circumstances.

Conscience is the ability to distinguish between morally right and wrong acts. The formation of a genuine conscience is dependent upon one's religious and moral training and is a reflection of Christ's teachings and the teachings of the Church.

When a Catholic is confronted with the prospect of divorce, he is alarmed at the possibility of such an action because, generally speaking, he is unaware of the ramifications of such a decision in terms of moral right and wrong.

Since the decision to divorce for a Catholic is often a choice between the lesser of two evils, an individual may conclude that his conscience is not a satisfactory guide to this major life decision.

The individual's conscience is a reflection of all that he has been taught regarding moral right and wrong. It is,

* For simplicity, the pronoun "he" is used throughout the book in all passages that could pertain to either sex.

3

in addition, a depository for many complex secular and non-moral attitudes which the person has assimilated as a consequence of being reared in a pluralistic society.

Therefore, while the conscience of a Catholic may be a legitimate guide in the matter of divorce, it is also subject to the adverse teachings of situation ethics which can confuse the issue. Not all marital conflicts need to end in divorce; and while an individual's conscience may suggest this action as a solution, it is far wiser for the person not to rely on his conscience alone because of the complexity and far-reaching consequences of such a decision.

It is recommended that, when one's conscience suggests to him the possibility of divorce as a solution to marital problems, he seek pastoral and/or family counseling as to the wisdom of such a step.

Conscience can be a valid guide when corroborated by a pastor's or family counselor's examination of the marital problem and when the decision to divorce has been indicated after all other alternatives have been explored.

With respect to divorce, when is a Catholic excommunicated?

A Catholic is not excommunicated just because he obtains a civil divorce. Such an individual remains in good standing as a practicing Catholic so long as he does not attempt to marry a second time according to the present teachings of the Church.

Excommunication is a term which is primarily applicable to past centuries rather than the present time. An individual who was a public figure in the world, or in government, for example, whose behavior defied and ignored the teachings of the Church and caused great scandal by adversely influencing multitudes of susceptible persons, was excommunicated.

Thus excommunication was a public repudiation of an individual who deliberately flaunted his antagonism and hatred of the Church by the life he led.

Today the words "excommunicated" and "lapsed" are frequently (but incorrectly) used interchangeably with respect to Catholics. They convey the fact that a person no longer receives the sacraments of the Church, nor has he any interest in participating in the Christ-like life.

Divorce does not specifically suggest that a Catholic is lapsed. There are Catholics who remain faithful to Christ and His teachings despite the human hardships that divorce imposes on them. Again there are other individuals who abandon, either temporarily or permanently, their allegiance to the faith because of divorce.

What is the status of a divorced Catholic in the eyes of the Church?

A divorced Catholic is not singled out by the Church in any way to distinguish him from all other Catholics. So long as he does not remarry, according to the present teachings of the Church, he may participate fully in the life of the Church.

There are instances where an individual may receive an ecclesiastical annulment after a civil divorce and then enter into another marriage. Other persons may misconstrue this situation and assume that the new marriage is an invalid one.

It is unwise, therefore, to pass judgment or assume knowledge of the circumstances surrounding the "second" marriage of a Catholic because the conclusions reached may be erroneous.

Naturally there are Catholics who have been validly married the first time, who have obtained a civil divorce, but do not (or cannot presently) obtain an ecclesiastical annulment and enter into a second marriage. Such a marriage is currently considered invalid.

The Church is most sympathetic with the plight of divorced Catholics who are in these circumstances. Many of these individuals send their children to Catholic schools and rear them in a totally Catholic milieu insofar as this is humanly possible under these conditions.

Although these Catholic men and women may not presently receive the sacraments, the Church is compassionate, and it is examining the dilemma of these men and women so that at some time in the future they may participate more fully in the life of Christ.

Can a divorced Catholic serve as an active member of parish groups such as: Altar Society, CCD teachers, councils, etc.?

There is no prohibition whatsoever in the Church which restricts divorced Catholics from participating in parish activities and any other Catholic community organizations. In fact, their participation is encouraged because it gives divorced Catholics, as individuals, a greater sense of self-esteem through serving their fellowman in a diversity of roles.

Divorced Catholics have been especially active in marriage and family life preparation courses in parishes. They are able to present realistic facts to young people about the consequences of impulsive decisions to marry, or entering into a marriage for the wrong reasons.

Panel discussions utilizing the resources of divorced Catholics are one mode of focusing attention on the need for competent marriage preparation for our young people, and at the same time, they enable the divorced Catholic to give of himself in a truly Christian way within the context of service to his fellow parishioners.

Is it a serious sin for a parent to neglect or refuse to pay child support and/or alimony where it was ordered by the court?

If a former mate or parent is capable of earning a decent living and he (in most instances) deliberately neglects to provide support funds for his children and alimony for his former wife (if it is ordered by the court), he is not fulfilling a responsibility according to the laws of God.

However, there are many complex aspects to this problem, both moral and legal.

Morally speaking in terms of past tradition recognized by the Catholic Church, it was (and is) the father's responsibility to provide the financial support for his children. It was (and is) the mother's responsibility to provide the day-to-day physical care and nurturing and emotional stability and love which gives the children a sense of security and enables them to grow into whole (psychologically mature) adults.

State laws have changed, and are still in the process of change, in order to embrace and recognize the powerful social changes that are emerging as a result of the women's liberation movement, the Civil Rights Act of 1964, and other subsequent legislation for equality. The philosophical and practical implications of this and future legislation indicates that there will be a trend to make both father and mother equally responsible for child support under the law.

In practical terms this will place an extraordinary burden on the woman because, in most instances, she is still responsible for the children's physical and psychological well-being in addition to their financial support.

This dual responsibility occurs in most cases because support ordered by the court and paid by the father is often inadequate. In addition, many fathers pay intermittently or eventually abandon the financial responsibility altogether. Hence the woman is left with almost insurmountable obstacles to face. In most instances, she is realistically unable to match her former husband's income and provide a lifestyle to which she and her children were accustomed in the past.

This inequity is unlikely to change in the future, despite legislation, due to the discrepancy between the man's responsibility after divorce and the woman's.

There are, of course, circumstances where a parent, or both parents, are unable to provide support for children after divorce. This may occur because of actual physical illness, accident, or serious psychological problems which make a sustained pattern of earning impossible. When such conditions occur, and are provable in a court of law, a man may be held liable for support of his children. This, of course, may be a temporary or fairly permanent situation. Then a woman is expected to provide both financial support and all of the necessary human care to sustain her children.

Refusal to pay child support can, in theory, be remedied by further court action. However, in reality, because of the time and money involved, most women usually rely on their own earning resources, or else they apply for some sort of governmental assistance.

When this situation is viewed in terms of the possibility of serious sin, it is advisable to explain the details of an individual case to one's confessor who can then offer an accurate and specific interpretation.

If the custodial parent deems the influence of the visiting parent harmful to the children's moral training, and the State refuses to restrain the visiting parent, what moral obligation does the custodial parent have in terms of removing the children from this adverse influence?

This situation is a very difficult one. The parent who has custody of minor children has a moral obligation to see that their religious and moral principles are not subverted by a hostile parent who may adversely influence the children. This parent, however, cannot do the impossible, and some situations call for endurance rather than alteration. The parent who has visitation rights can enforce them, but the parent who has custody has the legal right to prevail in matters of religious and moral training.

In order to prove that a hostile parent is damaging the children's moral training, the parent who has custody may approach this problem with the help of a psychologist or family counselor. The parent can discuss the problem with a counselor, who is sympathetic to the situation, and explain some of the visible manifestations of confusion that are likely to occur.

For example, an adolescent may be torn between two parents who are attempting to instill contrary moral or religious attitudes. The adolescent may refuse to attend Mass and receive the sacraments. He may also be confused and manifest his ambivalence by a poor scholastic record or destructive social behavior. The adolescent may thus refuse to see the parent for a combination of reasons since there is a high probability of friction and misunderstanding between them.

A custodial parent in this situation may wish to work through a lawyer. Sometimes a lawyer can bring both parents together with a family counselor present who can point out to the parents a course of action that is in the best interests of the child or adolescent. If a visiting parent is reasonable, he may agree to refrain from adversely influencing the child or adolescent. On the other hand, he may be immature and vindictive and not genuinely concerned about what is best for the child or adolescent.

In certain instances, a return to court might alleviate the situation, but since this is such a nebulous area of human behavior, it is wiser to attempt to bring all the parties together and agree to some constructive course of action outside of court. Also, because court proceedings are time consuming and expensive, it is frequently not a realistic course of action for the custodial parent, who is more commonly the mother and generally limited, financially speaking.

Sometimes a parent may consider an alternative to petition the court to move from one jurisdiction to another where the visiting parent does not have access to the minor children. In this way serious spiritual and/or psychological harm can be averted.

In other instances, some women (it is more often the mother than the father) simply move to a different part of the country and attempt to reestablish their families elsewhere. This is one method of escaping duress and adverse influence by a parent who is trying to destroy everything a custodial parent is attempting to build for the children. In these cases, a woman might forfeit child support payments. She may also have further litigation if the father demands his rights of visitation.

Every case of this nature needs to be reviewed on an individual basis because of the unique facts involved. Almost always, there is a measure of heartbreak because if one parent is deliberately destructive in terms of the children's moral life, it is very difficult for the other parent who has custody to extricate himself of the legal complications that can arise after divorce.

This does not mean that the custodial parent should not seek help. By all means, he should make the problem known to those who can help correct the situation. Sometimes even a tyrannical and destructive parent will end his harmful influence on minor children when he realizes that their moral allegiance is elsewhere.

Is it acceptable (not a sin) for a mother to release custody of the children to the father because she cannot cope with the problems involved with raising them alone?

The decision to transfer custody of minor children from

the mother to the father (or other guardian) is a serious one. Generally speaking, such a decision is outside the sphere of moral wrongdoing, unless a parent intentionally gives the minor children to an irresponsible or disturbed adult who will harm them in some way. If a mother is contemplating such a change in custody, it is recommended that she obtain pastoral and family counseling first.

There are multiple and continuing stresses on a woman who is rearing children alone. She is generally forced to live a spartan life with the children because her earnings are not comparable to her former husband's income. She is required to make instant solitary decisions with respect to all areas of the children's lives. They depend on her in every way when they are very young, and a woman may feel that there is no one to whom she can turn for moral support.

A woman in these circumstances may be lonely and depressed. She may drift into affairs or alcoholism or drugs. She may become debt-ridden through no fault of her own. In essence, her whole life seems at times to be "impossible," and she may feel that she cannot cope with her children. She may then begin to look upon them as a burden even though she may love them dearly.

It is at these crisis times that a woman may contemplate releasing her children to the custody of the father or another guardian. This is a consideration that must be examined cautiously and in the light of what is best for the future development of the children.

A woman should seek immediate counseling to relieve her of the crisis symptoms she is experiencing which appear to compel her to make such a decision. She should call a Family Life Bureau or a Catholic social service agency or any appropriate government agency which offers practical assistance to her. These agencies can often direct a woman to a specific organization that can help her. Once her crisis symptoms have been evaluated, she

11

can, with the help of a counselor, examine her motives for a contemplated custody change. There is no one answer that is applicable to these situations.

Sometimes a woman will find that she believes she can cope better with life and her children after the initial problem has been solved or alleviated to a degree. For example, a woman may feel that she cannot cope because she has a serious health problem. A counselor may point out to her that her health condition is temporary and may be improved. Thus she may wish to make some conditional arrangement, which is not legally binding, with her former mate for the care of her children while she is temporarily indisposed.

To give up completely the legal custody of one's children would suggest that some permanent, irreversible condition has occurred in the mother's life. This might be in the nature of a health problem. Apart from this factor, almost all other problems facing a woman can be dealt with so that a mother can retain custody.

Naturally if a woman wishes to remarry and the prospective husband does not want to assume any obligation for her children, then she may consider giving the custody of the children to the father.

Although there is no sin involved in a transfer of custody, this is a problem that should be discussed with a priest, first of all, and then a family counselor. There are so many complex psychological, spiritual, emotional, and health implications for the children that no responsible mother would make a hasty decision in this matter even though she has multiple continuing problems.

There are many church and community resources that she can utilize to help her with the rearing of her children. She should certainly exhaust all of these possibilities before contemplating any change of custody because of the serious problems that could ensue for her children.

Does the Church have any specific or well-defined position on custody of the children—whether it is more beneficial for them to be brought up by the mother or father—dependent on individual circumstances?

The Catholic Church emphasizes the importance of marital love and unity because it provides the foundation for wise parental guidance.

When husband and wife are divorced, the Catholic Church does not suggest in any way that one parent is superior or inferior to the other in matters of child rearing.

Through its social and family agencies, the Catholic Church attempts to assist a mother and father to fulfill individual responsibilities to the children. The Church's influence on the family life after divorce is a voluntary one in the sense that the parent who has custody is free to participate in its religious and social activities.

There are circumstances when one parent is a more appropriate mother or father than the other parent. That is to say, he or she is capable of the sustained and arduous efforts that are required for solitary child rearing.

Sometimes a mother or father is not genuinely interested in the children. He may enjoy the fun time occasions but be negligent as far as moral guidance, love, companionship, discipline, and the ability to make and carry out long-range plans for the benefit of the children.

Traditionally the courts have generally awarded very young children to the mother unless there was some prearranged agreement whereby the father was granted custody. Adolescent children are often asked which parent they prefer to live with, and the courts tend to acknowledge and honor these requests.

Tradition, however, is now changing, and with the wave of equality that is sweeping over the courts, men are asking for and obtaining custody of minor children in cer-

13

tain instances. The court, however, still decides custody on the basis of what appears to be best for the children.

In circumstances where the father is given custody, the mother may wish to relinquish this privilege because she may be entering into another marriage. Or she may have a very demanding job and not be able to find anyone to care for her children.

There are many ostensible reasons why a woman relinquishes custody voluntarily, but there are only a few genuine reasons why she actually does so. Aside from serious health problems, a substantial number of rational explanations may be given, but often they hide the truth that some women do not want the responsibilities that child rearing imposes on them. Or they may be honestly incapable of sustained responsibilities because they have serious psychological problems which would eventually affect the children adversely.

When the custody of children is contested, and mother and father equally fight for them, there may be a variety of decisions depending on the individual circumstances of the case. Minor children are generally awarded to the mother even though the father may ask for custody. Unless there is some extraordinary evidence against the woman which indicates that she would not be a responsible mother, this custody award is followed.

Exceptions to this trend are becoming widespread. A father may have some unique life circumstances of unusual advantage (not necessarily material) which may provide a clearly beneficial life for the children in contrast to that which can be provided by the mother.

For example, a mother who has a criminal record of drug addiction may not be granted custody; but if she can later prove rehabilitation, and she wants to take on the responsibilities of motherhood, the courts tend to recognize this prerogative and may alter the earlier custody arrangement.

DIVORCED CATHOLICS

Our society still functions very much in a pattern which allows the woman maximum fulfillment of herself as a human being through her responsibilities as a mother. Society, at the same time, makes it enormously difficult for the average woman who is divorced to earn a comfortable living for her children and herself, despite regular child support. This is the great dilemma in the life of a divorced mother.

A father may love his children as much as the mother does, but the powerful customs of our society do not change in one generation. The male role is primarily that of the breadwinner, the leader, and he earns love and respect from his children (even after divorce) chiefly through his fulfillment of these functions. His ability to be a moral guide and companion to his adolescent children is possible only if there is some sort of practical cooperative arrangement with his former wife. One of the reasons the male influence tends to ebb and wane in the life of adolescents is that the father (more often than the mother) tends to enter into another marriage, and his interest begins to fade.

Sometimes a father will insist that his love and devotion is constant to his adolescent children, although he has remarried and may have a second family. While this may be true in some unique circumstances, the actions of the father speak louder than any words he may utter.

If the mother is sincerely attempting to rear the children within the context of the Catholic faith, then inevitably adolescents will begin to examine and analyze the actions of the father. They will understand that "Do as I say, and not as I do" is the key to understanding their predicament. The same is true if the roles are reversed: the father has custody and the mother has remarried.

The Catholic Church realizes that there is no "ideal" post-divorce situation. There are some circumstances where one parent is clearly more altruistic and benevolent, while the other parent is quite irresponsible. However, in cases of divorced Catholics where both mother and father attempt to live morally upright lives afterwards and guide their children according to Christian tradition, the Church maintains no position on which parent is more beneficial in terms of custody.

The Catholic Church suggests that a willingness to consider what is best for the children in terms of their human development and eternal salvation be used as a guideline in the conduct of both parents.

If a mother cannot cope with her children alone, and the father's influence will turn them away from or against the Church, what is the alternative?

A mother in this predicament should seek immediate pastoral and family counseling. The decision before her in terms of the law is whether she will relinquish custody of her children because she is unable to cope with them, or whether she will retain custody and somehow find the resources within herself to struggle along and help her children to become mature adults.

A mother cannot ignore the father's legal rights to custody of the children if she relinquishes them, regardless of any religious problems. A civil court does not settle religious disputes between parents who have opposing views. The court determines who will have responsibility for the children if one parent voluntarily gives up his legal custody. Next in line is the other natural parent unless that parent can be proven unfit. Generally speaking, the courts do not determine unfitness on the basis of any religious controversy between mother and father.

Therefore, if a woman is seriously considering giving up her children, she should understand that the children's father will probably be awarded custody.

If, however, a woman can prove that the children's

father is an unfit parent, then the court may consider any other close relatives on either side of the family who demonstrate their fitness by their past lives and their willingness to accept this responsibility. Should no close relatives be available, it is possible that the children might become wards of the court.

A mother should, however, examine her feelings and all that she means when she says that she "cannot cope with her children" before giving them up. This is a decision that will affect her for the rest of her life. If she is giving them up because she believes that she will have an easier or more comfortable life, it might be wise for her to express her innermost feelings and anxieties to a priest or a qualified counselor in a Catholic social service agency.

So many times a woman reaches a critical impasse and thinks she cannot go on, when, in reality, she is searching for emotional support and encouragement. She may need a temporary respite. Even a day away from her responsibilities as a mother may give her feelings of hope for the future.

Therefore, counseling is really essential when a woman is faced with such a serious decision. Her primary consideration should be the present and future lives of her children. A counselor can help her to understand that the sacrifices she makes for her children are manifestations of love that they need in order to become whole (psychologically mature) adults. This achievement and goal should be kept in mind when considering a change in custody.

If an ex-mate is really a bad (irresponsible and immoral) parent, do I have an obligation to tell my children the truth about his or her character? Or should I be a hypocrite and tell my children to love and respect his father or mother?

Much depends on the age of the children or adolescents

and the ability of the custodial parent to deal with the subject in a reasonable and compassionate manner.

Children do need to be protected from a parent who will have a deleterious psychological, spiritual, or physical effect on them. They do need protection in instances where the parent is disturbed (regardless of whether he has been identified as psychotic), and children should be entitled to have their moral and religious training upheld by a visiting parent.

Unfortunately the legitimate rights of the children receive secondary consideration in terms of civil law because the law gives priority to the natural parent (who does not have custody) with respect to visitation rights. These rights cannot be taken away unless a parent is proved to be unfit. There is, additionally, a disparity between the legal interpretation of an unfit parent (as far as moral responsibility is concerned), and a moral interpretation according to the laws of God.

Therefore, when a parent wishes to disclose the truth about a genuinely immoral or psychopathic or immature parent, he may be misunderstood by other adults who erroneously believe such a disclosure is an act of vindictiveness.

The truth is naturally a major consideration because of the well-being of the child. But a wise and loving custodial parent needs to weigh truth against the possibility of another kind of psychological and spiritual harm to minor children. That is, when a child hears the worst about an absent parent, even though such a disclosure may be true, there is the strong likelihood that the child will retain some serious emotional scars. He may develop a fear or hatred of a parent, or a fear or hatred of anyone who is of the same sex as that parent, thus distorting future relationships. These negative emotions need not be "planted" in the heart of a minor child even though a par-

18

ent does not wish to be hypocritical about the absent parent.

On occasion, there is a compromise solution wherein a child discovers the truth for himself about the nature of his parent's character.

Aside from situations wherein there is high risk to a child's life (when, of course, he should be literally removed from the irresponsible or immoral parent), specific jeopardy in terms of moral subversion, for example, should be examined with the aid of a pastoral or family counselor.

A custodial parent needs to use common sense and discretion, and he needs to understand that such personality disturbances do constitute a real risk to minor children. Therefore, although he should not paint a villainous portrait of the other parent, he should be alert to opportunities for limited social contact with such a parent so that the child can gain an independent awareness of the deficiencies of a father or mother.

Are divorced spouses still morally responsible for each other's welfare, either spiritually or physically? Even after one of them remarries?

In one sense, a divorced mate is responsible for the welfare of his former spouse. This interpretation is, however, to be construed in the general sense that we are all our "brother's keeper." In other words, if a divorced person knows that his former mate is having some serious difficulty such as health or financial problems, then it is possible that he should offer some assistance even if that person can only offer moral support and prayers.

Despite this Christian concept of concern for each other, this attitude may be unrealistic in practical terms. For example, there may be so much bitterness, and so many emotional problems may recur if there is any link between the two people, that it may be wiser, if practical assistance is needed, to offer it through an intermediary.

Such assistance may be refused even though it is desperately needed. Or the reverse situation may occur. A husband or wife may revert to psychological dependency on a former mate, and it may be almost impossible to sever the emotional tie if it is once again revitalized through the offer of some kind of aid.

When one of the mates remarries, any recurrence of a former relationship, even in terms of friendship, places a serious strain on the second marriage. A policy of non-interference should be followed unless the circumstances are extreme, and even then the matter should be discussed with a pastoral or family counselor before a decision is made.

An individual may still have strong feelings of affection for a former mate, and these feelings may be mingled with other ambivalent emotions. He may show his concern for a former mate by prayers for his well-being. However, once again, such attitudes may become obsessive and hide personality problems of the individual who feels "morally responsible." This may be a mask for guilt feelings, particularly in instances where a former mate was an alcoholic or drug addict.

In any situations where a former mate feels doubt about his responsibilities to a spouse no longer present, there should be some sort of pastoral or divorce counseling so that the individual understands his true feelings and also understands the nature of being his "brother's keeper" in these special circumstances.

If one party of a divorce believes he is still married in the eyes of God, how should this individual accept the "remarriage" of the spouse?

The remarriage of a spouse should be accepted as a fact of life by the other former mate despite his religious convictions. The second marriage is legal and is recognized in the pluralistic society in which we live.

Although an individual man or woman may adhere to the religious conviction that the sacramental bond of his marriage is intact in the sight of God, there is every good reason, from the point of view of mental health, for him to relinquish the past and accept the reality of a second marriage of a former mate. One of the problems in such a situation, from the counselor's point of view, is that such an individual who cherishes this valid religious conviction may unwisely depend on it so that he uses it as a false obstacle to rebuilding a new life for himself.

The moral and legal dichotomy can be accepted by an individual who has genuine religious convictions. But in instances where a man or woman has serious emotional problems resulting from the divorce and remarriage of a former mate, the individual may be wrenching this religious belief out of context because he still has a strong need to identify with a former mate. Believing that one is still married in the eyes of God falsely nourishes this illusion.

A man or woman in this emotional predicament needs counseling to distinguish his religious values from the pluralistic world in which he lives. Some reconciliation between the two must be made so that the individual is motivated to live a constructive life in the present and refrain from living in the past.

How should a family (relatives) deal with a divorced member (including immediate family, for example, one's brothers and/or sisters)?

When a member of the family (a brother or sister or close relative) has gone through the ordeal of divorce, he needs to be treated with warmth, consideration, and respect.

The initial impact of divorce often causes family members to judge one or both partners adversely in such circumstances. Thus at family gatherings there may be considerable strain and even overt animosity. An in-law may judge the former spouse to be a serious sinner or label him with other derogatory names.

Even when a divorce is uncontested, and one of the parties actually wished to dissolve the marriage, there is still much emotional upheaval. In cases where there is a contested action and a battle over children and/or property rights, both former spouses suffer a great deal of turmoil. This is true even though one partner may have deliberately caused the break-up of the marriage through serious personality problems. He is disturbed and needs divorce counseling to come to terms with himself before a new life can begin.

Therefore, anyone close to a person who has experienced this traumatic life crisis should attempt to be helpful and non-judgmental although he may have private thoughts to the contrary.

When a former mate is immature and/or seriously disturbed, he is more inclined to attempt to make a better life adjustment in the future if he is not criticized or berated for past actions.

Usually this process of self-awakening and identification of traits that may have caused the dissolution of a marriage may be identified through the process of post-divorce counseling. A family member can give practical assistance to another relative in this situation if he encourages post-divorce counseling. Naturally counseling cannot and should not be forced upon an individual. He needs to come to this decision independently.

The recently divorced person must reassess many aspects of his life. He is extremely sensitive to relatives who may seem to wish to make decisions for him.

Hence the most compassionate attitude to take is to offer helpfulness and assistance in whatever way is acceptable to the newly divorced person. He needs to find a new inner direction before setting forth on an independent life.

Is scandal still a sin? If so, when is one guilty of it with respect to divorce?

Scandal may be defined as any act or series of acts which offend the morality of the social community.

Catholics today live in a pluralistic society in the United States. It is not homogeneous or representative of only one religious tradition. Our country mingles many religious traditions and cultures including atheism and agnosticism. Despite this collection of heterogeneous influences in contemporary society, many Americans like to think of our society as one which was founded on Judeo-Christian principles.

In truth, our culture has drifted away from its original religious heritage. Our heterogeneity has deteriorated to an amoral culture.

Compare a substantially homogeneous society, for example, the England of King Henry VIII's time. The country then was primarily Catholic, and there was no separation of church and state until Henry VIII threatened to set himself up as the head of the church in England.

The all too familiar series of marriages and divorces of Henry VIII may be considered as scandalous and sinful. These acts occurred within a specific social framework. That is, Henry VIII was a public figure capable of giving scandal. His behavior adversely influenced multitudes of people. The society was not heterogeneous, and there was no clearly defined separation of church and state.

Hence Henry VIII's actions were offensive to the social community and public morality of his time. Finally his behavior represents an amoral philosophy of life which even to non-believers of any specific religious tradition constitutes a hazard, since this amorality suggests an "acceptable" life pattern.

Scandal, therefore, within this context is not likely to occur today or to be defined as sinful since our country is not homogeneous, and no one set of rules (except legal laws) can be imposed upon the general population (including Catholics).

In our pluralistic society, scandal becomes a nebulous (although real) concept. Moreover, the current permissive standards which prevail today have tended to make many individuals "scandal-proof." That is, there appears to be no behavior that might conceivably be shocking. While this would naturally differ from one individual to another, a general consensus would tend to interpret "scandal" in terms of a specific set of circumstances in a given community. Therefore, while one cannot say that scandalous behavior does not exist today, one can say instead that scandal must be interpreted within a very selective context because of our prevailing amoral milieu.

There is one exception to this sociological interpretation. That is, scandal with respect to parents/adults and children, especially as it is related to divorce among Catholics, does exist.

Parents are morally responsible to God for their actions. Any adulterous or perverted relationships that either parent may be involved in does scandalize their children and adolescents. A man or woman who plans to divorce his mate specifically for the purpose of marrying another person, with whom he may be living, is guilty of scandal.

The vulnerability of young children and adolescents to the harmful and/or amoral behavior of either or both parents is frequently manifested in disturbed or delinquent behavior by the child or adolescent. Sometimes a child or adolescent may be unable to form a right conscience in matters of sexual morality, and even general ethical principles, because one or both parents choose to scandalize them.

The deleterious effects of scandal in this sense may not be manifested for years until the child become an adult. At that point the repercussions of scandal may be reflected in personality disturbances, a loss of religious faith, and an inability to sustain mature inner-directed behavior in a relationship with the opposite sex.

Any man or woman, therefore, who is concerned about scandal in relation to divorce should consult with his confessor and/or pastoral counselor.

Can a divorced Catholic date if he does not intend to marry?

We explored this question pro and con in our book *The Divorced Catholic*, because it is certainly a vital issue.

There are pastoral and family counselors who can present reasonable arguments for each side of the question. It is not an issue which can be answered definitively since each case of dating is unique in certain respects.

For example, the divorced man who escorts a woman to a large impersonal social function may provide himself with an attractive companion in a situation where it is mandatory for him to appear with a wife or feminine companion.

The same circumstances are true for a woman. She may need an escort for a specific social occasion, and it is unlikely that a priest would construe this social relationship as dangerous or inadvisable.

The difficulty with any dating situation after divorce is that it is impossible and unrealistic to compartmentalize human emotions and deny their existence. A man or woman may need an escort for one social occasion, but this does not mean that regardless of good intentions, an individual may not yield to his human feelings and become seriously attracted to someone of the opposite sex.

An individual "may not intend to marry again," but human emotions may easily become more urgent and ignore this good intention, and then the man or woman finds himself enmeshed in a complex pattern of rationalization.

He may not necessarily become involved sexually, but the longer the friendship goes on the more likely it is that human feelings will overwhelm one or both parties. Thus an individual will be in the dangerous position of being compelled to decide whether to enter an invalid marriage (probably) or give up the practice of his religious faith.

This torturous experience can be avoided only by adhering to a decision which is difficult and often misunderstood, not only by the general population, but by many Catholics as well. To insist that one is not susceptible to human temptation in such circumstances constitutes a refusal to face reality. When a divorced Catholic is seriously contemplating and weighing the risks in this situation, he should seek supportive pastoral counseling in order to come to terms with his ultimate decision.

The problem of dating should be further examined in view of the possibility of a person who is seeking an ecclesiastical annulment after obtaining a civil divorce. It is possible, for example, that a divorced Catholic may not know whether or not he can have his marriage declared null and void in the light of the more comprehensive interpretation of psychopathic personality deficiencies of one of the former mates. Such lack of due discretion cases, as they are called, are now considered manifestations of lack of personal consent, and hence are declared null and void.

When an individual initially begins dating on the assumption that he is not eligible to marry within the Church, and subsequently learns that a valid marriage is possible because of the receipt of a nullity of marriage, he may alter his attitude depending on the personal circumstances of his case. Hence a counselor can offer only a general answer with respect to dating. As a specific alternative, a family counselor may recommend individual pastoral counseling. Such pastoral counseling serves to illuminate and emphasize the sacramental nature of marriage to those individuals who may be eligible to make a valid marriage in the Catholic Church after divorce.

If remarriage after divorce is not possible, whom am I hurting by having an affair? Maybe I will be a more loving human being and a better parent to my children if I have some sexual release and adult companionship.

This reasoning is subjective and seems to provide a temporary "solution" to a complex and far-reaching problem in the individual's life. Contemporary situation ethics promotes such a "solution" because it deludes the individual's conscience into believing that his personal values take precedence over an objective moral law of God.

While one in such circumstances may find temporary sexual appeasement, he does so at the price of stifling his conscience. He pretends that the universal moral law of God does not exist. Inevitably there is disillusion and disappointment because one or the other person in such an affair will end it to move on to another liaison. Since there is no binding moral commitment to each other and to God in such an alliance, the ease with which one or the other may slip out of a liaison is obvious.

To assume that one may be a better parent because one has a mistress or lover is equally fallacious. Self-deception is at the heart of such a relationship, and sooner or later children realize that the parent is dividing his attention between them and a lover.

Contrary to popularized notions that children adapt to "anything," children may become seriously disturbed because of parental "arrangements" where there may be one or a steady stream of partners. This is a demeaning experience to children, and it confuses them. Their self-esteem, their moral conditioning, and their future adult personalities are adversely affected by parental liaisons.

When a person is willing to accept the fact that he has deluded himself about such relationships, it is possible for him to be aided by a pastoral and/or family counselor to live a loving life on other terms.

Does a divorced Catholic have to advise a priest of his status in confession?

A divorced Catholic is not obligated to divulge his status to a priest in confession. However, it is recommended that any man or woman who has the opportunity to cultivate a priest as a regular confessor should do so following his divorce.

Such a confidence enables the priest-confessor to better understand the problems that the divorced Catholic brings with him. There are those individuals who feel they can unburden themselves of many doubts, anxieties, and guilt feelings in the privacy of the confessional, whereas they would feel inhibited from doing so if they were to have a face-to-face encounter with the same priest.

This confidential and trusting exchange is literally good for the soul. The confessor can appreciate the spiritual and emotional difficulties that the divorced person may have in a specific area of life. He can comprehend more fully the nature of the penitent's sexual temptations and transgressions, or his need to depend on alcohol or other pseudo-relief measures. This intimate rapport between a confessor and divorced Catholic is possible only when an individual trusts that he will not be criticized and condemned in a manner which will destroy his spiritual or human progress.

Thus understanding is a key factor. If a divorced Catholic goes to confession to a variety of priests, or for one reason or another is unable to find one who projects a capacity for understanding, then there is no practical reason why he should explain to each new confessor that he is divorced. This is a very individual matter.

Usually in the first year after divorce the individual wishes to make a new start in life, and he needs many different kinds of assistance and encouragement.

A priest-confessor can help the man or woman who is considering the abandonment of his religious faith following divorce. He can help those who have succumbed to serious sin by encouraging these individuals to accept Christ's invitation to a life of grace.

Regardless then of the individual's attitude toward his religious faith, a priest-confessor can help the divorced Catholic to strengthen his relationship with God.

How should a divorced Catholic prepare for confession?

Reconciliation with God is now emphasized as a distinctive characteristic of the sacrament of Penance. The penitent needs to feel hope, and he needs, above all, to feel that he is once again reunited with God after confession.

The sacrament of Penance consists of: confession, contrition, and satisfaction or reparation for one's sins.

It is customary for the penitent (a divorced Catholic is like any other penitent) to prepare for the sacrament by praying and examining his conscience prior to confession. In this prayer before confession, a person asks God to help him to know his sins and confess them, and to amend his life.

A thorough examination of conscience is essential for a good confession. Most prayer books that include a section on the sacrament of Penance provide a detailed collection of questions pertaining to each of the Ten Commandments. These questions enable the penitent to recall his offenses against God as well as any offenses against the precepts of the Church. The penitent must also recall to mind the duties of his state of life. For example, a divorced Catholic might examine his conscience with reference to his responsibilities as a parent. Sins of omission and commission should both be included in this examination of conscience.

Finally the individual must recall whether these offenses are mortal or venial sins. Thus during confession, the penitent is obliged to distinguish mortal sins by stating the specific circumstances surrounding a given act, and the number of times such an act was committed. It is not necessary to confess venial sins, although it is desirable to do so.

After an examination of conscience then, the individual must be truly sorry for his sins. He should make an act of contrition based on his love of God. This sorrow for sins should be related to the penitent's love of God, rather than his fear of hell, for example. While this motive is a natural human motive, it lacks the supernatural yearning for God which makes the act of contrition more perfect in the sight of God.

Subsequent to an act of contrition, the penitent must have the intention to amend his life. That is, he must be determined not to commit sin again, instead of the imperfect amendment which means that the individual may try to avoid merely one specific sin against God.

The divorced Catholic may have special problems with respect to confession. He may have neglected to practice has faith for a long period of time. That is, he may be a lapsed Catholic. Or he may have made a sacrilegious confession, and presently he wonders what steps are needed to effect a reconciliation with God.

If there has been any long interval or absence from the

sacraments, and a Catholic wishes to return to the practice of his religious faith, he needs to explain the circumstances of his lapse from the Church to a priest in confession. For example, a person may have entered into an invalid second marriage and subsequently have been divorced. Or he may have been living with someone without benefit of marriage, and the affair has now ended. There are many reasons why a divorced Catholic may have neglected to practice his religious faith.

The critical point is that he has now decided to return to God. The penitent may go to confession, but he must explain the nature of his lapse in terms of specific offenses against God. Such an explanation does not have to be complicated. The penitent need not be unduly fearful of condemnation. What is required is his sincere determination to return to God and amend his life.

In such circumstances, the divorced Catholic will often be helped by his confessor who may ask specific questions in order to understand the reason why the individual abandoned the practice of his religious faith. If a priest is convinced that there is genuine contrition and a desire to make reparation for the past, then absolution is given.

When a divorced Catholic has made a sacrilegious confession in the past, and wishes to effect a reconciliation with God, he must tell a priest specifically that his last confession was sacrilegious (because of deliberate concealment of a mortal sin). He is required to repeat all the serious sins confessed at the time of the sacrilegious confession, the original concealed mortal sin, and any other mortal sins committed in the interim between the bad confession and the present confession.

Sometimes a divorced Catholic may wish to make a general confession if he has been absent from the faith for a long time. He may find an especially opportune time for such a general confession at a retreat. Then an individual can review his past life with the retreat-confessor,

31

and the penitent can go into detail about problems which may have kept him from returning to the faith sooner.

Frequently the penitent feels tremendously unburdened and cleansed of his sins, and he is receptive to the grace of God, and determined to live a life according to the teachings of Christ.

Amendment or reparation for sin is the final element of the sacrament of Penance. If there is any realistic possibility for rectifying wrongs done to another person, for example, the individual can set about correcting the situation. Amendment includes not only the prayers given by the confessor, but all those practical acts which can right situations of injustice to others.

Thus the sacrament of Penance is an invitation to reconciliation with God and the Christ-like life. It is a vehicle of grace which strengthens the individual in time of temptation, and it reminds the penitent that his eternal destiny is earned by the right exercise of his intelligence and free will.

Would a Church declaration of nullity release the moral responsibility of the spouses for each other?

A declaration of nullity is an ecclesiastical annulment which declares that a marriage was null and void from the beginning because of an impediment at the time the parties gave this consent. It was thought that consent would constitute a valid marriage.

As explained in another answer, the moral responsibility of a former spouse is a complex issue. It cannot be defined without knowledge of a specific set of circumstances. Therefore, a former spouse who has feelings of moral responsibility toward an ex-mate should consult with a pastoral or family counselor who can help him examine the situation and determine his responsibilities.

A declaration of nullity is really peripheral in this issue

because each of us is, in one sense, morally responsible for those individuals who come across our paths in life and ask for help. That is to say, each human being, regardless of his marital status, must attempt to live a Christlike life in terms of charity and compassion for others. One does not need to have a distinctly identifiable moral or legal relationship with another human being in order to live according to this Christian principle.

Much of the hidden motivation in such a question lies in the likelihood that one mate secretly wishes to continue some sort of relationship with his former mate no matter how tenuous.

A woman formerly married to an alcoholic, for example, will feel that she is morally responsible for his behavior long after the divorce. Usually such erroneous assumptions are based partly on guilt feelings and on her inability to construct an independent life for herself. Such a woman or man, depending on the circumstances of the case, needs pastoral or family counseling in order to understand that he must look ahead toward the future and not use the motive of "moral responsibility" as a crutch to cling to a past life which has ended.

How does a Catholic apply for a marriage investigation if the pastor of his Church refuses to cooperate?

A Catholic who is having serious marriage problems and is seeking an investigation for purposes of obtaining a nullity of marriage is not limited to any one priest for assistance. He may find a sympathetic and compassionate priest in a parish removed from his own geographical location. A man or woman is not limited in any way in his search for a priest who can help him in these circumstances.

Briefly, a priest will ask the man or woman for a detailed written history of his courtship circumstances and marital problems, to be submitted along with a copy of the civil marriage license and final decree of civil divorce annulment. Then a priest will present this written document with his own attestation of the person's integrity and moral responsibility to the local marriage tribunal for further investigation.

Explain the contractual nature of marriage according to the Catholic Church. How does it differ from a civil contract?

Christian marriage is an intimate, interpersonal partnership between a man and a woman whereby the spouses, through personal consent, mutually bestow upon each other and accept from each other those rights and obligations which are directed to the procreation and education of children; to the promotion and fulfillment of mutual help and service; and to the total communion of life and love.

God is the author of Christian marriage. In practical terms, this means that marriage as a sacrament transcends any human limitations and is not subject to human, that is, civil or legal decrees.

There are certain characteristics of Christian marriage which make it unique and different from any civil contract:

1) The Catholic Church teaches that the marriage contract is a sacrament. One cannot exist without the other. Moreover, the bride and groom administer the sacrament themselves. The priest acts as an official witness of the Church so that without his presence the marriage would not be recognized as valid. There are exceptions to this general rule, and these exceptions have to be approved by the local Ordinary.

2) Christian marriage is a covenant which binds husband and wife to each other for the purpose of fulfilling

all of the responsibilities involved in child-bearing and rearing.

3) Christian marriage is a unique contract in the sense that consent to this contract is personal. No human power can substitute this consent for the consent of the individuals involved. That is, neither parents, nor civil, nor Church authority can agree to offer the consent in lieu of the individual man or woman. Hence, free and knowing consent (due discretion) of both partners must be voluntarily given; otherwise, there is no valid marriage.

4) According to the teachings of the Catholic Church, marriage is a unique contract in that it is God alone who sets forth its special nature. Men and women are free to consent or refuse consent to enter into marriage, but they are not free to change the nature of the contract.

Christian marriage differs from civil marriage in its contractual nature in several respects. First of all, Christian marriage is characterized as a sacrament.

Secondly, it is a contract which is "until death do us part." That is, according to the laws of God, no human authority (the state) can dissolve a valid Christian marriage. This means that although the Church may recognize a legal dissolution of marriage, it does not recognize a dissolution of the sacramental bond of marriage.

A civil marriage differs from Christian marriage primarily in the sense that it is similar to other legal contracts. That is to say, it has a beginning, and it may be terminated according to the wishes, via legal action, of one or both parties.

A civil marriage contract does not recognize the sacramental nature of marriage, nor does it acknowledge God as the author of marriage.

Since there is a separation of church and state according to the Constitution of the United States, Catholics are obliged to obtain a civil license to marry in accord with the laws of the state in which they reside (or marry).

35

In addition, they will participate in a marriage ceremony according to the rites of the Roman Catholic Church in order to acknowledge God as the author of marriage, and thereby attest to their religious faith in the doctrines and moral principles for which it stands.

If I had it to do over again, I would not go through with a divorce. Why do I feel this way?

There are many reasons why a man or woman may have had a change of attitude about divorce after he has gone through this experience. For both sexes there is a tremendous adjustment to a new life pattern. Each must learn to function as an independent human being. The transition from interdependence to solitary independence can be traumatic. Some men and women do not honestly make a satisfactory adjustment because they lack the resourcefulness, initiative, and physical and psychological stamina that is required of them.

It is possible that a mate for such a person was a parent substitute, and the immature dependency he brought to marriage was fateful in causing the marriage to collapse.

Dependency then is one of the main unconscious reasons why an individual may regret divorce. He prefers the security of an unhappy marriage but realizes this truth only in hindsight.

Lack of a regular sex partner and absence of sexual fulfillment is another reason why a person may regret divorce and wish for a return to his old relationship. Although he may have abundant opportunities to fulfill his sexual needs outside of marriage (apart from the moral implications), there are a substantial number of people who yearn for a stable, predictable sexual relationship which does not have to be clandestine. Some of these feelings are related to attitudes of dependency upon a former spouse. They are very real frustrations, and the individual who regrets a divorce may be unconsciously desirous of sexual fulfillment without the related problems that he may have had in his former marriage.

A woman frequently discovers additional reasons for regret. She is not only compelled to be independent, but she must prove it by economic resourcefulness. Her ability to earn a living may be hampered by insufficient education, her duties to minor children, and considerations of age and work experience.

A divorced person may long for the security of a former marriage by deliberately "forgetting" the realistic problems which caused the divorce. In other words, he may construct an elaborate rationalization of his former life and decide it was not so bad after all when he compares it with the reality of the daily pressures he faces as a divorced person.

Men and women with lingering memories of regret are inviting emotional problems for themselves by refusing to face reality. Post-divorce counseling with a priest and/ or a family counselor may be of great value to them because it will help to build a bridge from the past to the present. Counseling will enable them to assess their lives as it is here and now and provide the supportive encouragement they need to relinquish the past and build a happier independent future.

Is my relationship with God changed for the worse because of my divorce?

The Catholic who has gone through a civil divorce may have an accumulation of guilt feelings mingled with shame, anger, fear, and generalized anxiety. Sometimes a Catholic feels that God is angry with him and that divorce is a "punishment" for a past misdeed. He may express fear (particularly since he faces multiple practical post-divorce problems) that his relationship with God may have deteriorated. He may experience powerful feelings of self-contempt and self-hatred and fallaciously assume that not even God could love him because of the mess he has made of life.

A Catholic's relationship with God is not altered by the fact of civil divorce. An individual's relationship with God depends on his attempt to do the will of God as it is known to him through the Ten Commandments and the teachings of the Church.

A person may feel a closer relationship with God when he participates in a retreat, for example. This occasion affords an individual the opportunity to unburden himself to a priest with respect to the state of his soul and his spiritual progress. A priest can reassure him that his relationship with God cannot be measured by his emotions which may mislead him.

A more intimate and comforting relationship with God is possible by frequent attendance at Mass and reception of the sacraments. As Catholics, we understand that Mass is the perfect sacrifice and is most pleasing to God our Father. Through the sacrifice of the Mass, he offers adoration and thanksgiving to God. He petitions the blessings of God upon his daily efforts, and finally participation in the Mass acts as reparation for sin. Regular reception of the sacraments is also another opportunity for the divorced Catholic to draw closer to God. The graces received from the sacraments of Penance and the Holy Eucharist enable a disheartened person to go forth with courage in his heart and meet his daily responsibilities in the knowledge that God loves him.

Any spiritual and temporal acts of mercy which one wishes to offer as acts of loving concern for his fellowman in the name of the love of God may further enrich the individual's relationship with God.

Meditation, spiritual reading, and prayer are other aids to intimacy with God our Father. It may be difficult for someone who is troubled and unhappy in his personal life to believe that God loves him personally as a distinct human being. At such times Thomas à Kempis, in *Imitation of Christ*, reminds us: "Do not be troubled and do not fear. Trust strongly in Me and have perfect hope in My mercy. When you think you are very far from Me, I am often quite close to you."

A HISTORY OF DIVORCE

In almost every society there has been some provision for divorce. From ancient to modern times divorce has been resorted to as a legal means by which the marriage relationship was dissolved, the property of the husband and wife was divided, and some plan for the education and maintenance of children was established until they reached adulthood.

Primitive pre-Christian societies valued a stable marriage no less than the more sophisticated Christian society that flourished later. However, the essential difference between pre-Christian and Christian marriage was that the former society did not necessarily consider marriage to be a permanent indissoluble union, while the latter society introduced the concept of indissolubility. This concept had serious repercussions in the subsequent history of divorce laws in civilized societies.

Some pre-Christian societies limited divorce and permitted it only under certain circumstances which will be discussed later. Most commonly, a man was allowed to divorce for his own reasons, which he did not always have to specify, whereas a woman was restricted in her right to obtain a divorce.

Because marriage was not a permanent relationship in primitive societies, the incidence of divorce was high. Among Semitic peoples, for example, a husband could repudiate his wife at will. A Hebrew man was permitted to divorce his wife with no formalities.

Neither ancient Jewish nor Arabic tradition recognized

the right of divorce for woman. Under specified conditions, however, a woman could file for dissolution of her marriage. Under Arabic tradition a husband was allowed the privileges of polygamy, and it was not until the time of Mohammed (570-632) that a man was restricted to monogamous marriage.

In contrast, Hindu society endorsed monogamic marriage, and it was considered indissoluble until death. There were exceptions to this rule: abandonment of a faithful wife, adultery by the wife, or serious offenses against a husband.

Chinese tradition was established on monogamic marriage, although concubinage was a recognized part of family life.

Pre-Christian societies virtually ignored woman as a human being with dignity and innate individual rights. A woman was little more than expendable chattel. She was totally dependent on the good will of her husband and her father's home from which she came.

The right to human dignity in marriage came to women only through the introduction of the Christian concept of indissolubility.

ROMAN LAW

Early Roman tradition encouraged marital stability, but the gradual decadence which ensued caused marriage to crumble as a social institution. A man could divorce his wife by simply giving notice to her. Mutual consent was common. While a husband's adulterous action was not considered grounds for divorce, a wife might appeal to the archon for divorce on other recognized grounds.

Prior to the decline and fall, Roman society frowned upon divorce, and it was only after a period of general decadence became established that divorce became acceptable, and even fashionable.

Under Roman law marriage was a civil contract, and there was no acceptance of the thesis of indissolubility. Judicial procedure was resorted to only if the partners did not consent to divorce by mutual consent. Obviously the partners had to reach a further agreement with respect to the division of property and the custody of the children.

Marriage was a temporary or loose partnership arrangement. There was a steadfast refusal under Roman law to acknowledge the Christian concept of indissolubility. Gradually, however, under the influence of early Christianity, Roman divorce law was altered, but the principle of dissolubility continued in effect.

Mutual consent was by far the most popular ground for divorce and it remained so for more than 500 years during the reign of the Byzantine emperors.

Modifications and additional grounds for divorce became effective under the Emperor Constantine. In 331 A.D. the Emperor permitted *divortium ex bona gratia* if the husband was away at war, providing there was no information about him for a period of at least four years. Other grounds were later added such as prenuptial impotence lasting two years after the marriage, capture as a prisoner, taking vows, entering a monastery, or accepting the rank of bishop.

In 542 A.D. the Emperor Justinian provided grounds for *divortium cum damno*. These grounds were treason, attempt on the life of the other spouse, adultery, acts creating the presumption of adultery by the wife (for example, going to the theatre or to public baths against the husband's will), abortion, adultery by the husband if committed with a married woman or in the common home of the couple, and for both parties: idiocy, leprosy, and insanity.

Marriage between adulterers was prohibited. An adulterous wife was punished by being required to remain celibate for five years. If she did not obey the restriction on marriage, she was publicly declared infamous.

Under Justinian's concept of divorce, there was a guilty and an innocent spouse, and this tradition evolved through canon law to contemporary civil law where it is only gradually being phased out by a no-fault divorce concept. Justinian decreed that grounds not explicitly included in the law were to carry with them specific punishments, ranging from forfeiture to the innocent spouse a part of the guilty spouse's property to celibacy for a specifically defined period of time. In other instances, banishment was the penalty imposed.

When a divorce was obtained by mutual consent, each spouse was ordered into a monastery or convent for the rest of his life. The property of the husband and wife was to be divided among the children and the monastery or convent. This punishment was so severe that public opinion forced it to be removed, and it was repealed twenty-three years later in 565 A.D. by Justin II.

CANON LAW

The doctrine of the Church concerning the teaching of indissolubility has a valid Biblical tradition, particularly in the new Testament writings of Matthew.

New Testament teaching constituted a clearly defined break with the Old Testament, which permitted divorce (Dt 24:1-4). This passage in the Old Testament states the existing law that allows a husband to repudiate his wife if something "indecent" is found in her. While this expression is nebulous, it aroused dispute as to what constituted grounds for divorce.

As in many pre-Christian societies, the women of Old Testament tradition were not allowed to obtain divorce. The husband, however, was allowed to issue a statement dismissing his wife and this in essence freed him of any obligation to her. In Deuteronomy (24:1), Isaiah (50:1), and Jeremiah (3:8) there is reference to a written document as a bill of divorce. The divorced woman was to be returned to her father's house, and could be given again in marriage (Dt 24:2).

Other marriage and divorce restrictions are noted in the Old Testament. A man who had violated a girl, whom he was required to marry, did not have the right to obtain a divorce (Dt 22:28-29). Similarly, a husband who had wrongfully accused his wife of impurity before marriage was forbidden divorce (Dt 22:13-19).

The New Testament introduced the teachings of Christ, and there is a significant break with the past. Christ allowed no exceptions. However, many scholars agree that the "exception phrase" in Matthew presents problems for Catholics in view of the later defined indissolubility characteristic.

That Christ condemned divorce has been pointed out by Biblical scholars; see Matthew (5:32, 19:3-9), Mark (10:2-12), and Luke (16:18).

The critical "exception phrase" dealing with fornication has been admitted to include adultery, and permits a simple separation but no remarriage. Admittedly, this Biblical passage was not adequately explained and remained obscure until an official declaration by the Council of Trent in 1563.

Canonical legislation concerning the doctrine of indissolubility was introduced by Gratian, a Camaldolese monk, who codified many of the early laws of the Church. He asserted that a consummated Christian marriage was held to be indissoluble and moreover was under the jurisdiction of the ecclesiastical courts. This declaration of indissolubility was set forth in the second part of Gratian's Decree (Decretum Gratianum) published around the year 1140 A.D. Although the Decree of Gratian was a private compilation of papers and legal norms, it later served as the nucleus for the development of legal codes.

Both the indissolubility of consummated Christian marriage and the authority of ecclesiastical courts were inferred from the sacramental character of marriage. In 1439 the Council of Florence officially confirmed these assertions. They were further reaffirmed by the Council of Trent in 1545-63.

In 1917 the *Code of Canon Law* again reiterated the Church's position on the doctrine of indissolubility. In part, it stated, "... A validly contracted and consummated marriage cannot be dissolved by any human power or for any reason except death" (Canon 1118). Canon law governing the examination of alleged invalidity for marriage is found in the fourth book of the Code, Canons 1552-2194.

Current scholarly legal studies with respect to the doctrine of indissolubility and the concept of a validly consummated marriage have included an exploration of the consent of the parties and its relationship to validity and invalidity. The concept that consent makes the marriage has been legalized in Canon 1081 which states: "The consent of the parties lawfully expressed between persons who are capable according to the law makes a marriage. No human power can supply a substitute for this consent.

"Matrimonial consent is an act of the will by which each party gives and accepts the perpetual and exclusive right to the body for the performance of actions which of themselves are apt for the generation of children."

The Second Vatican Council has enlarged the vision of consent. In "Gaudium et spes" (No. 48, "Joy and Hope"), the Second Vatican Council stated: "The intimate partnership of married life and love has been established by the Creator and qualified by His laws. It is rooted in the conjugal covenant of irrevocable personal consent. Hence, by that human act whereby spouses mutually bestow and accept each other, a relationship arises which by Divine Will and in the eyes of society is a lasting one. For the good of the spouses and their offspring, as well as of society, the existence of this sacred bond no longer depends on human decisions alone. For God Himself is the author of matrimony, which is endowed with various benefits and purposes."

Taking into consideration the above development, recent decisions from the Sacred Roman Rota, the high court of the Church, have broadened the basis by which certain marriages may be annulled. The pronouncements of this Court, although not infallible, are norms which may be followed by other Church Courts throughout the world.

In a decision handed down by Monsignor Felici of the Rota on December 3, 1957, reference was made to the necessity of having a critical or discretionary capability for the consent to marriage.

Canon law further recognizes advances in psychiatry regarding personality deficiencies related to the inability to consent. A psychopathic personality deficiency prevents a person from fulfilling essential marital obligations and insuring the God-given goals of marriage.

Historically the Roman Rota defined the problem of psychopathic personality deficiencies within the narrow context of the individual's ability to give rational consent at the time of the marriage. The impact of research in psychiatry and the behavioral sciences has afforded the Roman Rota an opportunity to examine in greater depth this rigidly defined thesis of rational consent.

A more profound understanding of the deficiencies of the psychopathic personality, within the context of consent, was arrived at by the Roman Rota after thorough investigation of the problem. Thus human consent at the time of marriage ("to know" the obligations of marriage) was not sufficient for valid consent, but rather consent was defined as the ability of the individual to understand and fulfill the essential obligations of marriage on a continuing and enduring basis. This sustaining ability is absent in the psychopathic personality, and he is incapable of such a commitment.

Thus a nullity of marriage invalidates such a relationship and gives an individual the moral right to enter into a valid marriage according to the teachings of the Catholic Church.

The impact of research in psychiatry, psychology, and the behavioral sciences has been especially persuasive not only on revisions and reinterpretations of canon law, but on the civil judiciary and legislative systems as well in the United States and other civilized countries.

Agitation for divorce reform has continued in a quiet, unspectacular way in many countries throughout Western Europe, England, and the United States during the nineteenth and early twentieth centuries. It is only in the latter third of the twentieth century that there has been the introduction of radically liberalized divorce laws in some parts of the United States and England.

Prior to the twentieth century a conservative tradition of divorce was maintained. Divorce was a stigma in secular society to a great extent, except among very wealthy people, whose wealth often enabled them to live apart from the repercussions of a divorce decision.

With the advent of the present century and the vast economic, sociological, educational, and political changes, including women's liberation, that have taken place, the impact of divorce and its continually increasing incidence in Western Christian society has come to be felt on all levels of society and among all religious groups.

UNITED STATES

The history of divorce in the United States during colonial times is necessarily fragmentary and incomplete. Puritanism was the prevailing religious philosophy of the early settlers, and as a result, the incidence of divorce was low. Revealing their kinship with England, the colonists viewed marriage as a civil contract, and not as a sacrament, with the exception of those colonists in Maryland who were Catholic.

The earliest divorce statistics are fairly modern and go back to 1870. In that year, there were about 11,000 divorces in the United States. This meant that one out of every 33 marriages would end in divorce.

Numerically the incidence of divorce has increased from 11,000 in 1870 to over 400,000 per year in the 1960s. The greatest number of divorces in a single year occurred in 1946 when 610,000 were on record. This figure represents the trend toward hasty World War II marriage and divorce.

Compare though United States Census figures since that time, and it is apparent that there has been a steadily increasing trend to divorce, notwithstanding an increase in marriage due to population growth.

Since 1970 the figures for marriage and divorce are:

Year	Marriage	Divorce
1970	2,159,000	708,000
1971	2,196,000	768,000
1972	2,269,000	839,000
1973	3,277,000	913,000

In 1970 one out of every three marriages terminated in divorce. In 1973 approximately one out of every 2.5 marriages ended in divorce. There is every likelihood that divorce will continue its upward spiral if there are no efforts to reverse the statistical facts of the past.

Since there is no national divorce law in the United States, it is not practical to enter into a discussion of individual state laws and their relationship to these statistics, but rather to offer a general commentary instead.

Traditionally, Judeo-Christian ethics and English common law have been the most powerful influences on the molding of the state divorce laws in the United States. Our laws reflect both traditions in their adherence to an adversary system and the concept of guilt and innocence in awarding divorce.

In the recent past, agitation for divorce reform has gathered considerable momentum, and certain states, such as California, have adopted a no-fault basis for dissolution of marriage. Women are no longer granted alimony, and it is an exception rather than the rule for such an award to be made in many states because of the trend toward equality under the law which assumes that a woman can earn her own living after divorce.

Mounting national divorce on all levels of society thrusts the burden of family disintegration upon churches as well as state and federal governments. Increased assistance to women and children via a great variety of state and federal programs indicate that they do not fare well financially, on the average, when they are compelled to face life without a husband and father. Divorce reform must realistically recognize that government subsidies are not the answer to equality of the sexes following the dissolution of a marriage.

Prospects for a uniform national divorce law appears to be inevitable at some time in the future in view of the increasing incidence of divorce and its nightmarish ramifications in terms of human devastation. A revision of divorce laws without a concomitant revision of marriage laws would tend to nullify whatever negative benefits to society might accrue from the former.

The formulation of divorce law and marriage law in the United States is presently very susceptible to the influence of the behavioral sciences. There may indeed arrive a time when diverse psychiatric, psychological, sociological, and medical-ethical concepts may become assimilated in such reforms.

CURRENT TRENDS

A general assessment of the history of divorce, particularly in the United States, would be incomplete without some reference to the radical changes in morality which have affected marriage and divorce since World War II.

As the influence of Judeo-Christian ethics has waned, a moral dichotomy has emerged distinguishing two essentially antagonistic positions regarding marriage and divorce. The ascendancy of the new morality has heralded the decline of traditional moral values which are fundamentally Christian in essence. At the heart of this upheaval is a denial of individual moral responsibility, and in its place is to be found situation ethics, a fashionable philosophical euphemism for total and systematic annihilation of Christian values.

Earlier in this chapter it was noted that the Roman Emperor Justinian in 542 A.D. introduced the concept of innocence and guilt in divorce proceedings. This historical interpretation has filtered down through the centuries and has been the prevailing theory behind divorce laws and in divorce courts throughout the world to the present time.

With the gradual decline of religious influence around the world, the traditional view of guilt and innocence in divorce proceedings is being replaced. The recent abolition of this concept and its replacement by the "no-fault" thesis based on situation ethics insinuates that no one is to blame, that two people are simply not suited to each other, and that there should be no guilt in terms of legal

51

penalties for either spouse in a divorce action.

Is it possible that such a legal "solution" constitutes a last ditch stand against total chaos in society? For no-fault divorce does not really diminish acrimony, nor does it rectify injustices of one mate to another. Instead the no-fault thesis is somewhat akin to the mother who appeared before Solomon and requested that a living baby be divided in half in order to be "fair" to both mothers who claimed maternity.

Moreover, the evolution of divorce reform codifying "no-fault" and making acceptable a thesis of "Neither mate is right or wrong" is an ominous portent of contemporary society's drift toward a conscienceless, or psychopathic, orientation toward life. Thus, in fact, no-fault divorce becomes an avowed repudiation of the Christian concept of individual moral responsibility for human acts.

Sophisticated interpretations of legislation are meaningless when a marriage counselor or a social worker is confronted with the reality of even one "dissolved" family: a wife-mother, husband-father, and children who are instantly liable to become enmeshed in the "gears" of state machinery due to their need for public assistance, anti-social behavior, delinquency, and a myriad of other related problems.

No-fault divorce is not a "clean" antiseptic approach to marital problems and dissolution. It is essentially superficial and ignores the festering malaise beneath the sterile, impersonal court-filed papers in a divorce action.

The malady hidden beneath the "solution" of no-fault divorce is available for scrutiny in any marriage counselor's office where he sees a cross-section of humanity which is largely unprepared to face the responsibilities of marriage.

Most marriage counselors, social workers, psychologists, priests, ministers, rabbis, and other professional people concerned with marriage and family life are seriously disturbed by the relationship between inadequate preparation or no preparation for marriage and a constantly spiraling divorce rate.

It is this combination of no-fault divorce and insufficient preparation for marriage that is so disheartening to a marriage counselor. Is it inevitable that hundreds of thousands of human lives will be dumped on the social scrap heap by a refusal of our legislators to recognize the need for marriage law reforms, including mandatory pre-marriage counseling and education, in addition to a need to acknowledge the Judeo-Christian principle of individual moral responsibility as a foundation for authentic positive change?

The full impact of current legislation is ominous in terms of greater confusion, personal delinquency, emotional disorders of adults and adolescents, an increase in suicide, and a collapse of family life with a visible trend toward total social chaos.

A just social order demands recognition and reinstatement of individual moral responsibility in divorce and marriage law reforms.

NULLITY OF MARRIAGE

The approach to nullity of marriage, or ecclesiastical annulment, has undergone vast changes in the United States since the Second Vatican Council. The average Catholic neither understands nor is informed of the proceedings of a nullity of marriage. And, in fact, it is only the individual whose marriage is in serious trouble (or has been dissolved in the civil courts) who becomes knowledgeable, and then under traumatic circumstances.

Moreover, young people of high school and college age are astoundingly ignorant of this vital proceeding because marriage and family life courses in Catholic schools and colleges may not make any reference to the subject at all. Or they may not require students to take such courses for their future life preparation. Thus it is only a minority of young adults in their late teens and early twenties, who have actual personal experience with annulment proceedings, who have any comprehension of its significance in their lives.

For most men and women the annulment experience occurs at a calamitous time in their lives: when a mate informs them that the marriage is over. They are suffering from multiple emotional lacerations, self-doubt, self-hatred, and confusion. Their marriage may have existed for over a decade, but it was an intolerable relationship, one which was endured year after year until one or both mates accept the reality of divorce. Then after civil divorce, one of the formerly married will decide to petition for a nullity of marriage through an ecclesiastical court or marriage tribunal.

For the divorced Catholic, a nullity of marriage appears to be the perfect solution to his problems. It gives an individual the moral right to enter into a marriage recognized by the Church by virtue of the fact that the first "marriage" was declared invalid, and therefore, null and void.

In the United States there are presently about 6000 nullity cases pending before various marriage tribunals. Although the number of ecclesiastical annulments has steadily increased in the past years, since the establishment of the twenty-three American Procedural Norms, there still remains a serious disparity between those Catholics who wish to receive an annulment, and those who actually do.

The fact that there are five million divorced Catholics in the United States, and only a small percentage of them have petitioned for an ecclesiastical annulment indicates that many major and controversial issues still exist and remain to be solved. Part of the solution to this problem lies in a consideration of revision of canon law. Another aspect is the need to educate Catholics about annulment proceedings and the sanctity of marriage as it applies to life in a pluralistic and anti-Christian society.

Despite the prevailing circumstances, the average Catholic can feel more hopeful about the possibilities of obtaining an ecclesiastical annulment because of a recognition of psychopathic personality deficiencies that may have relevance with respect to the invalidity of his marriage.

"'Gaudium et spes" is the Magna Carta of the new regulations concerning marriage. In this document, the Second Vatical Council stated: "The intimate partnership of married life and love has been established by the Creator and qualified by His laws. It is rooted in the conjugal covenant of irrevocable personal consent. Hence, by that human act whereby spouses mutually bestow and accept each other, a relationship arises which by Divine Will and in the eyes of society is a lasting one. For the good of the spouses and their offspring, as well as of society, the existence of this sacred bond no longer depends on human decisions alone. For God Himself is the author of matrimony, which is endowed with various benefits and purposes."

In contrast, the complex hedonistic society in which we live promotes a divorce-oriented, morally irresposible philosophy of life. If one marriage does not work, the cynics suggest, the next one (or the next one after that) will surely work. Reverence and compassion for human life has eroded so that the wreckage of human life via divorce destroys the innocent while the psychopathic personality remains unscathed and unconcerned. The doctrine: "What God has joined together, let no man put asunder," has now been scrutinized under the light of an individual's incapacity to fulfill essential marital obligations and insure the God-given goals of marriage.

The early inflexible restrictions have yielded to a more comprehensive and compassionate interpretation of those psychopathic deficiencies in an individual which prevent an authentic consent and ability to live in a sustaining, monogamous partnership with a husband or wife.

As human life has grown more sophisticated in our materialistic society, and as civil law has shifted toward a "non-moral" or "no-fault" basis systematically demolishing Judeo-Christian ethics, the moral law as interpreted by the teachings of the Church has reexamined the constellation of pressures that exist within each human personality and manifest themselves specifically in an inability to assume the continuing obligations of marriage.

Thus men and women who have deficient personalities do not necessarily appear to be "abnormal" or "peculiar" in any way in fairly casual or impersonal relationships. It is only when a relationship has existed over a long period of time within the intimacy of marriage, for example, that the collection of immaturities identified as psychopathic come to the fore and strain the marriage relationship to the breaking point.

In the past, the Roman Rota examined and evaluated psychopathic personality deficiencies only in terms of the individual's ability to give rational consent. However, in 1967 (Lefebvre, July 8, 1967), the Roman Rota decreed: "Among some psychopathic personalities, although not strictly ill, there is verified truly a pronounced disturbance of faculties from which flow the following consequences: namely, a true defect of election or a defect of a conscious free determination to a certain object with the ability to choose another."

The Roman Rota determined that such an individual cannot really give his consent because he is not capable of fulfilling the marital obligations involved in the contract. At the same time, the other mate is not receiving the essential object of this contract which is irrevocable personal consent. Hence, the validity of the marriage contract is defective. The psychopathic personality is thus distinguished by his incapacity to give irrevocable personal consent and to assume the marital obligations implicit in this consent.

Father Timothy O'Connell, Director of the Family Life Bureau in Los Angeles, explained, "The key words in the interpretation of a valid marriage are community of life, partnership, and the ability to give, take, and compromise, and to be unselfish."

Father O'Connell, who serves on the Los Angeles Archdiocese Marriage Tribunal, commented, "A lack of due discretion essentially comprises the wide range of psychopathic behavior which is the basis of many marital failures today. These individuals cannot relate to another human being or sustain a permanent monogamous relationship in marriage."

The ability to judge, to distinguish between "knowing"

(cognoscere) and the ability to carry out what "knowing" connotes (suscipere et assumere), that is, to undertake and fulfill the obligation of marriage in terms of community of life and love and the ability to give and take are vital aspects in determining the invalidity of a marriage.

The absence of this ability is ascertained only after husband and wife discover that one or both cannot relate to each other ("I don't think we ever really loved each other"), that there is an inability to form this unique community ("We don't have anything in common"), to make the sacrifices essential to marriage, and to commit themselves to a permanent and exclusive right to sexual intercourse with each other ("I never told you I would be faithful").

The Roman Rota in a series of decisions has explicitly stated that "the union of a person who cannot bind himself or be bound to the rights and obligations of marriage is invalid."

Father O'Connell said, "When a man or woman is seeking an annulment, the individual usually goes to his parish priest to talk over his problem. For that matter, a person is not restricted to his own parish. He or she can look for any sympathetic and compassionate priest.

"A priest will often ask a woman (60 percent of the cases in the Los Angeles Archdiocese are initiated by women) to write out in detail a history of her marriage, including the first meeting of the couple, the dating history, engagement, the wedding ceremony itself, the early years of marriage, when the first serious difficulty occurred, and the break-up of the marriage."

Father O'Connell emphasized, "Each case must be examined on its own merits. When one or both parties is unable to form this basic community of life and love, then we refer to these cases as 'lack of due discretion' cases."

Once a person has completed a detailed history of his marital problems, the petitioner then presents this information to the local chancery office through the priest who testifies to the individual petitioner's personal integrity.

Father O'Connell said, "Witnesses, of course, are needed to corroborate statements that a petitioner makes in his written marital history. Close relatives, friends, or people who were present at the wedding may be appropriate witnesses. Unlike a civil proceeding, "all are voluntary witnesses."

What if an ex-mate will not cooperate?

Father O'Connell explained, "Sometimes we will phone a former husband or wife to obtain suitable information. If an individual hangs up on us, or refuses to cooperate, this may indicate one aspect of a disturbed personality.

"What we try to do is to gather a profile of the husband and wife and the marriage relationship itself. The essential question is: Was there a marriage here in the first place? We rely on psychological and/or psychiatric evaluation. Both parties or one of the parties may be required to take the Minnesota Multiphasic Personality Inventory and a personality disorder test such as the Mooney or Taylor-Johnson evaluation in addition to a clinical history.

"When one of the mates refuses to cooperate with the petitioner and attempts to impede the investigation, this in itself suggests the likelihood of a personality deficiency."

There is one critical difference between the more rigid interpretation of a valid marriage in the past and the current Church position. Formerly the validity of a marriage was determined solely on the basis of proper consummation which was subsequent to this consent. When a marriage was celebrated with the proper consent, followed by physical consummation, it was very difficult to obtain a decree of nullity.

Father Clifford Parker, Associate Director of the Matrimonial Tribunal in Los Angeles, pointed out that now the more comprehensive interpretation is accorded to recognize the personality deficiencies of an individual. Thus although an individual may be physically capable of consummating the marriage, he may be psychologically incapable of assuming the obligations implicit in a sustained marriage relationship.

This psychological incapacity reveals itself in the basic information provided by the petitioner and is verified by witness and by expert psychological evaluation.

For example, the Church now recognizes the characteristics of a psychopathic personality outlined by Dr. Hervey Cleckley in *The Mask of Sanity*. Dr. Cleckley is Clinical Professor of Psychiatry and Neurology at the Medical College of Georgia, and he is Chief of Services, Psychiatry and Neurology at the University Hospital in Augusta.

Some of the characteristic traits of this personality disorder include:

1) Superficial charm and good intelligence

2) Absence of delusions and other signs of irrational thinking

3) Absence of nervousness or psychoneurotic manifestations

4) Unreliability

5) Untruthfulness and insincerity (wrenches the truth to fit the social situation)

6) Lack of remorse or shame

7) Inadequately motivated antisocial behavior

8) Poor judgment and failure to learn by experience

9) Pathologic egocentricity (selfishness) and incapacity for love

10) General poverty in major affective reactions

11) Specific loss of insight

12) Unresponsiveness in general interpersonal relations

13) Fantastic and uninviting behavior with drink and sometimes without

14) Suicide rarely carried out

15) Sex life impersonal, trivial, and poorly integrated, promiscuous

16) Failure to follow any life plan (drifter)

Because of the fact that so many of these traits can be interpreted as "normal" in certain situations—normal people do lie occasionally; they may consider themselves first before others once in awhile, etc.—the Marriage Tribunal relies substantially on the expert interpretations provided by a psychologist, psychiatrist and/or marriage and family counselor.

Many of these psychopathic individuals, Dr. Cleckley explains in his book, reveal unusual charm and persuasiveness. This is one of the reasons why a man or woman marries one of them. They appear to be normal, and it is only under the day-to-day intimacy of marriage and the stresses that accompany it that the psychopathic personality reveals a pattern of inability to live in a community of life and love.

Invalidity of the marriage thus in these circumstances is focused on the individual's incapacity to assume and sustain the obligations and responsibilities of marriage.

Father Parker, who is a canon lawyer, stated, "It is this incapacity which nullifies a marriage."

Father O'Connell added, "In cases of this sort, frequently the husband and wife are unhappy from the beginning of the marriage. Maybe the wife feels in her heart that she made a mistake even on the honeymoon, but she says nothing about it. Usually the normal partner tries to stick it out until some crisis or series of crises compels him or her to make a decision about the marriage.

"They may be married for fifteen years and have four or five children. They may have tried marriage counseling, and one mate is doing all the work to salvage the marriage while the other mate is completely indifferent. These people can still try to obtain an annulment on the grounds of lack of due discretion because of the likelihood of psychopathic deficiencies of a mate."

Father O'Connell explained, "The judge in cases of nullity must come to a decision of moral certitude. This means that the decision does not exclude all fear of error, but rather that the opposite opinion (valid marriage) in no way seems probable."

Father Parker summarized the steps in an ecclesiastical annulment proceeding. He said, "They comprise a *Petition* or request by one party to investigate the marriage for nullity. This request is submitted through the local parish. When the request is received by the Matrimonial Office, it is scrutinized for evidence and plausibility. If the request appears to be substantial for nullity, the Office will contact the parties to the marriage, plus qualified witnesses, who will be required to testify concerning the facts of the marriage.

"In addition, if one or both parties ever has been hospitalized for emotional illness, then evidence may be gathered from the proper authorities. The parties and the witnesses will be required to present these facts before a board of review at the Matrimonial Office. This board usually consists of three persons: two priests and a lay civil lawyer. Once the evidence is heard, this board will hold a consultation, and the head of the board will make a decision either for nullity or for validity. After the decision, the facts of the case must be drawn up in written form before the matter can be executed."

In cases of extraordinary circumstances requiring appeal to a court higher than the local diocese, more time may be required because of its complexity.

"However, generally speaking," Father Parker said, "the average uncomplicated case may be processed in about one year's time."

Due discretion, therefore, is the critical factor in an individual's ability to contract a valid marriage.

63

Father O'Connell said, "The Roman Rota has learned over the years that there are people who are incapable of living together in marriage because of pathological egocentricity. They lack the ability to give and take.

"The concept of valid marital consent is intertwined with due discretion just as invalidity is related to lack of due discretion."

The Roman Rota defines due discretion as the ability to undertake and fulfill marital obligations. Individuals who have deficient personalities, and who are identified as psychopaths or morally immature, cannot "undertake and fulfill" the duties of marriage.

There are innumerable Catholics today who are facing marital dissolution because of conditions beyond their control within the framework of deficient personality of a mate. Many men and women are reluctant to approach a parish priest, or any priest, to inquire about an annulment; or they may believe erroneously that their marital problem is hopeless and incapable of solution.

An ecclesiastical annulment (nullity of marriage) may be the solution to an individual's problems regardless of the length of his marriage. But he must take the initiative in bringing his case to the attention of the proper authorities.

A nullity of marriage then establishes the fact that no valid marriage did exist, and the petitioner who is granted the annulment is morally free to enter into a marriage which is recognized by the Catholic Church.

PETITIONER'S STATEMENT

PRELIMINARY STATEMENT OF A PETITIONER
CONCERNING THE NULLITY OF A MARRIAGE

A case must be started by the initiative of the party (or parties) to the broken marriage.

To begin the procedure, the petitioner must make a preliminary statement. The statement includes the allegations that form the basis of the claimed nullity.

If possible, please type out the statement of the case. Otherwise, write it out on ordinary paper.

OUTLINE FOR STATEMENT OF THE CASE

1. Name, address, telephone number, and parish of the petitioner. (If the petitioner is a woman, give name used at present, and maiden name.)
2. Religion; date and place of baptism of petitioner.
3. Name and address of the respondent. (The respondent is the other party of the marriage that you are petitioning as null and void.)
4. Religion; date and place of baptism of the respondent.
5. Date and place of marriage ceremony (or ceremonies, if more than one in the same marriage).
6. State whether civil divorce has been secured (when and where).
7. Reason for the asserted nullity of the marriage.
8. Facts in the case before, during, and after the marriage ceremony.
   a) *Meeting*—How and when did you start dating? What things happened that you now feel might be pertinent to your petition?

65

b) *Engagement*—How did the courtship develop into an agreement to marry? Was there any force involved?

c) *Ceremony*—How did the preparations—the choice of wedding attendants, the drawing up of a guest list, the rehearsal for the wedding, the ceremony itself, the reception, the honeymoon, etc., go?

d) *Cohabitation*—How did your life together go? When did the difficulties begin? What gave rise to them? What led to the first serious difficulty?

e) *Final breakup*—What brought it about? After how long? What means, if any, were used to effect a reconciliation?

9. Proofs: Witnesses—names, addresses, and telephone numbers of persons who can corroborate the allegations made in this preliminary statement. Documents, letters, affidavits, diaries, etc., if available.

Kindly date the statement and affix signature.

IMPORTANT: THE PRELIMINARY STATEMENT IS TO BE SUBMITTED BY THE PARISH PRIEST OF THE PETITIONER ALONG WITH THE PRIEST'S RECOMMENDATION.